# INSTAGRAM MARKETING

*The Ultimate Guide for Social Media Success*

## Copyright 2019 by For Side Hustlers

## All rights reserved.

This content is provided with the sole purpose of providing relevant information on a specific topic for which every reasonable effort has been made to ensure that it is both accurate and reasonable. Nevertheless, by purchasing this content you consent to the fact that the author, as well as the publisher, are in no way experts on the topics contained herein, regardless of any claims as such that may be made within. As such, any suggestions or recommendations that are made within are done so purely for entertainment value. It is recommended that you always consult a professional prior to undertaking any of the advice or techniques discussed within.

This is a legally binding declaration that is considered both valid and fair by both the Committee of Publishers Association and the American Bar Association and should be considered as legally binding within the United States.

The reproduction, transmission, and duplication of any of the content found herein, including any specific or extended information will be done as an illegal act regardless of the end form the information ultimately takes. This includes copied versions of the work physical, digital and audio unless express consent of the Publisher is provided beforehand. Any additional rights reserved.

Furthermore, the information that can be found within the pages described forthwith shall be considered both accurate and truthful when it comes to the recounting of facts. As such, any use, correct or incorrect, of the provided information will render the Publisher free of responsibility as to the actions taken outside of their direct purview. Regardless, there are zero scenarios where the original author or the Publisher can be deemed liable in any fashion for any damages or hardships that may result from any of the information discussed herein.

Additionally, the information in the following pages is intended only for informational purposes and should thus be thought of as universal. As befitting its nature, it is presented without assurance regarding its prolonged validity or interim quality. Trademarks that are mentioned are done without written consent and can in no way be considered an endorsement from the trademark holder.

# Table of Contents

Introduction .......................................................... 5
Chapter 1: "Insta-duction" to Social Media Marketing ............................................................ 7
Chapter 2: Diving into the Insta-Details .......... 26
Chapter 3: #GrowYourFollowing ..................... 49
Chapter 4: Insightful Advice ............................. 71
Chapter 5: Marketing Success Within Your Reach ................................................................. 94
Conclusion ........................................................ 114

# Introduction

Congratulations on purchasing *Instagram Marketing: The Ultimate Guide for Social Media Success* and thank you for doing so.

Social media. It's more than just a platform for sharing images and videos. It has evolved into a powerful marketing platform that – with the right strategy – can propel businesses to greater heights than they ever thought possible. Instagram is one example of such a platform that has presented many businesses with new opportunities and possibilities. Marketing strategies and techniques which were not possible several years ago are not only possible but *doable* now, thanks to the available tools on the platform.

Social media has completely changed the way brands and customers connect with each other. No more are companies cold, distant entities who do nothing more than churn out products for sale. With Instagram, your business can be more than just a company who cares about a sale in the eyes of your customer. With Instagram, your business can become a storyteller, a content creator, a visionary, a creative thinker, problem solver, artist, and more.

Customers no longer want a business that merely exists to sell them the products they want or need. These days, customers *expect your business* to make a lasting impression on them, and they want to see this happening through your social media campaigns. To successfully market your business on Instagram, you need to craft your content to fit in with the context of the platform, and you're going to have to do it with creative, out of the box thinking, innovative approaches, and the strategies you're about to learn.

There are plenty of books on this subject on the market, thanks again for choosing this one! Every effort was made to ensure it is full of as much useful information as possible, please enjoy!

# Chapter 1: "Insta-duction" to Social Media Marketing

You know what they are. You use them every day. Maybe even several times a day. They're literally *everywhere* across the internet, and there's not a single ad campaign these days that is not going to mention some kind of social media platform that encourages its users to get connected with. Here's a quick question for you:

*Do you know ANYONE these days who's NOT on social media? Or anyone who has never even heard of what social media is?*

The answer? Highly unlikely. This is the digital age we're living in, which means technology is inescapable. Anyone who has the means has a smartphone, or device of some sort which will allow them to connect to the digital world. The next time you're out walking the streets, look around you. Or ride the trains and subways to work. How many people seem to be glued to their mobile phone screens? You wouldn't have enough fingers and toes left to count them all. We are a generation that is addicted to our digital devices, and along with it, social media applications. That is because social media apps today are the easiest and most convenient way for people to keep in touch even if they may be halfway across the globe.

*Facebook. Twitter. LinkedIn. Instagram.* The big guns of the social media space. So strong is their dominating presence that you'll be hard-pressed to find someone who has never heard of these platforms before. Billions of people all over the world have at least one social media account which they are connected to. Which makes *this* the very reason you're going to now rely on social media marketing, *specifically Instagram Marketing,* to take your business and personal brand to the next level.

## Changing the Marketing Space Forever

Social media marketing has dramatically changed the way businesses and companies manage their communication with their clients. Ever since it started taking the world by storm, one user at a time, social media has completely revolutionized the way businesses market and advertise themselves. In fact, social media has changed the world to a point where if your business is not taking full advantage of the social media tools, you're going to be left behind. *Way behind* and that is something no business can afford to do.

## The Nuts and Bolts of Social Media's Workings

Social media applications were initially designed to be used by the mass public but seeing as how there is so much potential waiting to be taken advantage of, these applications have adapted and evolved to accommodate the business side of the spectrum. Here's why social media today is the mightiest power tool every business has. Compare social media to the traditional, old school way that businesses used to market themselves and reach out to consumers. One thing will be strikingly clear, and that is the old-school approach could *never* reach out or connect to customers the way that social media can. Social media marketing has taken over the business world to such a degree that most of us can't even remember the last time we used one of those conventional ads on television, radio, and newspapers to get our information. The business world simply has not been the same since, and it is time that all businesses learn how to take advantage of this extremely powerful tool.

Truth be told, conventional radio, newspaper, and television ads are simply not effective anymore. They are no longer the primary means by which audiences get their information from. It is the age of the internet where everything is online, everything is immediate, and almost everyone is accessible with just a few clicks of the mouse. Because the internet plays such a major role in the way our world is run, social media today is making just as much of an impact and it has become one of the quickest, most approachable methods businesses have at their disposal of connecting with their clients.

But if you think about it, is there really such a massive difference between traditional marketing and social media marketing?

Not entirely. In fact, social media marketing is, technically, still marketing. Except for this time, the difference is all the tools and techniques of marketing have been modified to accommodate social media platforms. They've also become optimized for these digital spaces, becoming more interactive, animated, and engaging. Companies are still using marketing to build their brand, promote their products, and create awareness. But this time, they are doing it on the internet space and connecting with the audience in the way the audience understands best.

Ad campaigns and new product launches were previously marketed through television, radio, and maybe even print mediums like magazines and newspapers. Today, they are now marketed first and foremost on social media. Social media allows for a connection with the audience in a way conventional marketing methods never could. The marketing method has changed the way we do business. Not only can companies and customers communicate with each other with a quick tweet or instant message and receive almost instantaneous responses. Social media marketing allows both companies and customers to make their voices heard and better understand one another.

**Social Media's Potential for Your Business**

Social media is a fantastic tool with tremendous potential for your business. Big companies and small companies all come with websites. Unfortunately, merely having a website these days isn't going to cut it. Company websites are great as a source of information about the company, but it doesn't have the right tools needed to be able to market or promote information that needs to be disseminated quickly. It certainly can't do it the way social media applications can. Which is what makes it such an effective marketing tool. One of those reasons why marketing efforts are a success on these platforms is because of the ability to connect in a deeper, more meaningful way to the customers; to build a *genuine relationship* with the customer that could be the beginning of lifelong loyalty. That is only the beginning of social media's potential for your business.

From a business standpoint, there are significant advantages to leveraging on social media's potential. For one thing, its relatively low cost, which is one of the biggest pros when it comes to social media marketing. Traditional marketing methods can be costly, while a lot of social media platforms are free or require a very minimal start-up cost. For a new business that is just starting to get off the ground and build a name for itself, this is an almost free (some advanced features are paid for), affordable tool that needs to build momentum and a steady customer flow on a budget. The wide audience reach, of course, goes without saying. No other platform out there will allow your business to reach millions and billions of customers around the world in a matter of *seconds*. We're talking about uploading content that is seen almost instantaneously by an eager customer who is waiting on the other side of the globe.

Yes, mere *seconds* is all it takes for your ad or business message to be conveyed on a global scale. Once it's online, it's there for all the world to see until you remove it. This content is what customers today prefer to interact with. The high level of interaction and engagement that you get with your audience helps to build much stronger brand loyalty and following, especially if your customers feel like they can relate to you.

The icing on the cake to this social media as a marketing tool is the high conversion rate to which traditional marketing methods could never even come close to. Plus, these platforms provide instant marketing insights, which are readily available. These built-in analytics tools in the social media applications allow companies to easily track their progress on a daily, weekly, and monthly basis, which in marketing, is essential to always know how a business is performing. With the help of these tools, companies can track their campaigns almost instantaneously because the information is constantly updated, and this is just another reason why social media marketing has so many advantages over the conventional marketing methods.

There are, of course, downsides to every scenario and social media is no different. Although most marketers would agree that the benefits of this marketing approach far outweigh the cons, every good business knows they must be prepared for anything. Part of running a successful business is doing your due diligence, and this includes looking at both the advantages and drawbacks of social media marketing as a tool. The risk and possibility of negative publicity is one example of a drawback. One wrong post is all it takes to bring your company's reputation tumbling to the ground. When your content goes viral, it is usually hard to control, especially if it is in a negative context. This could substantially damage your company's image.

Then, there's the time that you need to invest in maintaining a professional and presentable social media platform. With the speed at which information travels these days, if you are not fast, you are left behind. It is as simple as that. If your company is having a product launch or is about to make a big announcement that could potentially draw in more customers, you better be able to Facebook post it, tweet it, YouTube it, or Instagram it if you want to remain relevant and current among your customers. Effective social media marketing requires that you spend a lot of time online constantly refreshing and updating your content. This can be a very time-consuming process, and since these days businesses are likely to have more than one social media account at a time, you're looking at spending a considerable amount of time keeping up with your social media content alone. You might even need to hire additional staff just to manage this side of your business, and extra staff means extra cost.

Anything that is online, no matter what security measures are in place, is always at risk of being breached or hacked. For every new security measure invented, there will be a computer hacker out there who has discovered a way around it. Social media platforms are no different, which is another one of the drawbacks you need to keep in mind. Finally, being on such a public social space means you can't run away from negativity. Negative users are hard to avoid. Haters are everywhere, and never more easily accessible than on social media platforms. That's the reality of it.

The key to getting the most out of social media marketing tools is to understand that marketing messages need to be tailored to fit each social media platform for optimum leverage. Social media platforms work differently from one another, and a good marketer needs to know that while they may be promoting the same message across several social media platforms, the messages need to be tweaked and tailored to fit each social media platform and take advantage of how that social media platform works best. Over the next few chapters, you'll discover everything that you need to know about what makes Instagram "tick", and how you can leverage all the potential it has to offer to drive your marketing efforts to greater heights.

Another secret to effective social media marketing? Two words: *audience engagement.* Despite all the fancy features, entertaining filters, and video content that can keep you hooked for hours, at the heart of it all, being engaged is what social media is based on. Connecting with people from anywhere in the world in the most efficient and convenient way. Businesses need to use the same approach.

**Using Social Media to Build Your Brand**

The immense potential of good branding is all around us. Thanks to good branding and effective marketing efforts, big-name companies like McDonald's, Nike, Starbucks, and more have become the business powerhouses that they are today. They may have already been big names to start with even before social media became a factor, but now they're unstoppable. That's the level you want to aspire to for your business, too.

A business needs to capitalize on building a brand effectively on social media or they will soon be forgotten and cease to even exist. Everything is fast-paced and constantly changing, and the consumer markets are no different from this. Branding is a key element to the survival of a business because it is how your customers identify with your business. Building a business' brand on social media is critical to the survival of the business moving forward.

The very heart and lifeline of businesses are in the hands of your customer base. The larger the customer base, the more the sales potential. Of course, we all know what happens when a business has *no customer base* at all. It won't be long before that business eventually becomes non-existent. The way to build relationships and enhance exposure among your target customer base is through social media platforms. Not only can your business interact with customers from all over the world, but you can now do so 24/7 if you want to, simply by logging into your social media site. Customers love the idea of being able to reach a business anytime, day or night when they want. When you feed into that need, they're less likely to look for it in your competitors.

A business will see success on social media when it delivers attractive, fun, attention-grabbing updates and postings. That's how your audience starts to recognize and more importantly, *remember* your brand. When you *give them something to remember you by.* Create content that is memorable and engaging, and share behind the scenes stories and sneak peeks whenever possible. There are thousands upon thousands of other business social media accounts out there, and if your business doesn't put in the effort to make itself stand out in the crowd, it is going to be lost among a sea of other businesses and emerging businesses.

To build a brand strong enough to withstand the test of time, your brand identity needs to be *perfect*. Everything from the choice of logo, the color scheme used in all the designs, and the kind of font and photography used, every detail needs to be perfect and carefully selected. Even more so when marketing on social media platforms where visuals (like Instagram) are everything, and it can either make or break a company's success. If the audience doesn't find your brand identity engaging and appealing enough, they simply move on to the next thing; you've already lost part of battle there.

Your brand is the face of your business, and just like you would in person, you need to put your best face forward if you want to make a good impression. Your brand is the face that represents a business. It always needs to be kept fresh and up to date. Audiences are never going to be attracted, or even remotely interested in a brand that looks out of date. Social media is a fast-paced, ever-changing environment where everything needs to be new, fresh, and interesting. In the time it takes to snap your fingers, your newsfeed has already refreshed with the latest, most relevant content. Audiences are always on the lookout for the next big thing. Your brand needs to deliver, or audiences are going to get tired of your "face" real soon and that brand and company will eventually fade away into the background and be forgotten. Getting your audiences' attention is one thing. *Keeping* that attention long enough to get your message across is a different story.

Building a successful brand identity on social media is not always going to be a smooth and easy road, but there are certain guidelines you could abide by to make it *easier:*

- **Your Strength Lies in Your Voice** - Your brand's personality should reflect in every message and post that is being put on your social media account. Think of your Instagram account, for example, as the voice of your business. What your voice should be saying is that you're authentic, genuine, and true to your brand. Find your voice, your style, and be consistent in the way that voice is delivered to your audience, so they will come to associate it with your brand. Put some long, hard thought into this before you launch. Oh, and avoid the trap of trying to copy another brand's voice and style of presenting itself on social media.

- **Don't Rush the Process** - Social media may be fast-paced, but that doesn't mean you should be. Avoid rushing because, in your haste to launch your brand, you could end up making a lot more mistakes in the long run. Remember how one wrong move can instantly bring your reputation crashing down? Launching something as crucial as the brand image you're going to present to the world is a long process, but it will pay off if you take it one step at a time. A lot of time, energy, and effort need to be invested prior to launching a brand if you want to present a strong front when the brand makes its entrance into the business world, and you'll be glad indeed you decided to play it safe.

- **Don't Cut Corners (Financially)** - Sound advice that new start-up businesses, in particular, should keep in mind. Don't sacrifice the face of your company in a short-sighted attempt to save cost, and this goes for bigger companies, too. Cost-cutting without thinking long-term is a sure way to fail. A business may be all about maximizing profit, but keep in mind that there are some things which are worth investing in. As the brand image of your business, because your company's brand is not just a short-term fad; it is here to stay. Invest in the present for a stronger future moving forward.

- **Going for Cheap Will Be Your Downfall** - Understandably, the cost is a big factor for all businesses. But again, there are some areas where you need to make an investment for the sake of your future. Generally, we gravitate towards the best, budget-friendly deal available, but when it comes to selecting a logo that is going to represent the face of your brand, that is exactly what you want to avoid. There are websites offering already prepared logos for sale for businesses that don't have the means to design ones themselves, but this is one temptation you want to steer clear from. Cheap logos are exactly what it is – cheap.

- **Change May Be Good, But Not Too Often** - Your content should be the one to change frequently, but not your image. Your brand image is how your audience and customer base identifies with you (just like McDonald's, Wendy's, or KFC) so in this case, consistency is the key. To avoid constantly changing your brand's visual image too frequently, it would be wise to invest a considerable amount of time on proper planning. Audiences are not going to respond well to a brand that can't even appear to be consistent in the choice of its brand image.

- **Engage and Keep on Engaging** - Say it once, and keep saying it a million times. *Always engage with your customers.* If they comment on your content, always respond and never ignore. Dismissing, deleting, or ignoring your customers on social media is a death sentence for your business, and a risk you simply can't afford to take. If the comments are positive, thank them and let them know they're appreciated. If the comments are negative, apologize, be sincere, and let them know what steps the business is taking to make the necessary changes. Speak to them as they matter. *Because they do.* They are the heart and soul of any business, and without your customers, there would be no business.

- **Only Useful Content** - A word of caution when posting content on your social media accounts. You want to post more than once a day, *but only post content that is useful.* Every piece of information and content that a business puts out there on its social media sites is another piece in the building block that forms the brand's image. Frivolous information that does nothing to strengthen your brand image is just going to be a waste of time. Content needs to be original, useful, and engaging, which isn't always easy, but it is necessary if you want your brand to have a strong presence. Before you hit the upload button, stop, pause, look, and relook at your content again. Review it once, twice, and three times if you must. Remember each piece of information needs to uphold and reflect well on the brand image

## What the Future of Social Media Marketing Looks Like

Social media's importance these days can neither be ignored or downplayed. It is important, and it will *continue* to remain important over the next several years and counting because communication is the bread and butter that allows a business to win and retain their customers. And what's a business without its customers?

The social nature of these platforms has made the audience more receptive towards the messages and images that a business puts out there on its social media pages. Crafted messages and interesting images peak the customer's interests a lot more than mass produced ads do. Try going back to the old ways of marketing and see if you can reach the same level of potential social media offers. There's going to be a *big difference.* Social media platforms are the link your business has been looking for to get that extra foothold you need to engage with your customers and build a strong brand image among your followers. If you're a new start-up, you simply *cannot afford* to pass up on the opportunity that social media is serving you on a silver platter. All the branding or great product range alone won't cut it anymore, and it certainly *won't do* to only focus on websites alone. People frequent social media sites a lot more than they do websites, and if you want success, you need to go where your audience goes.

The future may change at the drop of a hat, but as of now, one thing's for certain. Social media marketing is here to stay. It is everywhere you look and to remain relevant in the world today, social media marketing is the *only way to go*. Social media platforms are no longer just for the purpose of posting an update here or sharing a hashtag image there. It has evolved into something much more crucial to a businesses' survival. It is a tool to gather firsthand knowledge about a business's target clientele through the way they respond to the social media messages put online. For a social media marketing plan to be effective, research is going to be a necessary part of the equations.

# Chapter 2:
# Diving into the Insta-Details

Many companies out there have successfully built a large following and customer base through their Instagram account. How did they do it? Well, the secret to successful marketing with Instagram depends heavily on the marketer's ability to be able to tell the company or business's story through nothing more than just images, videos, stories, IGTV, and short descriptive captions and hashtags.

Before we launch into Instagram and its inner workings, there are a couple of things to keep in mind *before* you begin marketing on this platform:

- **Guideline #1 -** Make your Instagram business profile available for public viewing, not private. Having a private account that restricts content from being seen unless the user is a follower of the account holder is a turn off for your customers. Even worse, many potential customers you might have attracted with your latest content is not going to be able to see it. Each customer that gets turned away (unintentionally) is a lost business opportunity. If you're wondering why it's such a turn-off, imagine feeling like you're being forced to follow the social media account just to look at one or two pieces of content you may be curious about. Customers are all about having choices, take that away from them and they're not going to be interested in your business.

- **Guideline #2** - Images on Instagram need to be vivid, colorful, and clear. Post images that are high quality, and avoid anything that is blurry and pixelated. Every image or video posted should be of high quality and as professional-looking as possible. Avoid simply snapping and recording anything just for the sake of appearing active on your social media account. To post successfully captivating images and videos, the content needs to tell a story. All images and videos that get posted on Instagram reflect your business, and they need to appeal to your target audience by being relatable. Let the content tell your business story.

- **Guideline #3** - Business does not mix with pleasure in this case. If you're a business owner or marketer with your own, existing Instagram account for personal use, create a new one that is purely for the business only. Mixing two together, while convenient to manage, does not project a professional appearance and you'll risk confusing your audience. How can they tell which content is personal and which is business-related? Likewise, do not post personal pictures on the company's Instagram profile, unless it is directly related to the business. Team-building or behind the scenes images are okay because it ties back to your company.

- **Guideline #4** - All the content you post on Instagram needs to be clear about what products or services your business is offering. It is important that the bulk of the content on Instagram be directly related to the business, so it is always reinforced with the followers what the business is selling or providing. Users and potential customers like to know exactly who they are dealing with and confusing content is just going to drive them away and to another competitor if they don't like what they see.

- **Guideline #5** - Be content-wise, and don't go overboard with your filters. Filters should help enhance your images and videos, not change them so drastically that they lose their appeal. You want to try and create a nice mix of content on your profile too, so your content doesn't appear too monotonous. Avoid sticking to images or videos alone. Mix it up! Your audience is diverse, and some audiences are drawn more towards image content, and some towards video content, and there are some who like to see both. To fully maximize your marketing potential, you need to create content that appeals to all these groups. And you do that by mixing it up.

**Welcome to Instagram**

Ever since they introduced their ad feature back in 2015, Instagram, like many of today's social media platforms, offers big and small businesses the incredible opportunities to reach both massive audiences as well as the targeted audience to connect with them, engage them, and ultimately convert them into customers. It's safe to say that Instagram ads changed everything, and marketers now have the ability to reach a niche segment of the population, Instagram ads have become an avenue for brands looking to increase their engagement and by extension, their profits, to the 500 million active users who use Instagram EVERY DAY.

Just look at some of Instagram's impressive user statistics as of 2019:

- More than 1 billion users who are active monthly (and counting).

- 500 million users and more who use Instagram Stories daily.

- More than 50 billion photos have been shared on the social media platform to date.

- More than 25 million business currently on Instagram.

- The potential advertising reaches through Instagram is currently at 802 million.

- Instagram videos get double the engagement of photos more so than any other social media platform.

As of July 2019, 110 million of Instagram's users are from the United States alone.

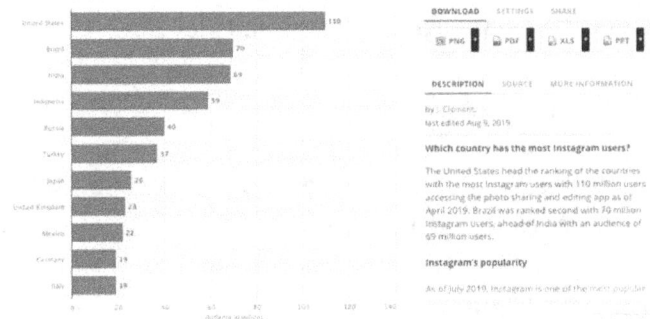

*Source: Statista*

However, the more and more brands join Instagram, the bigger the competition and the harder it is to stand out in a person's feed. To effectively stand out on your customer's newsfeed, you need to create content that goes the extra mile. When you think you've done a great job, ask yourself, *can this be better?* You need to keep pushing your boundaries and constantly improve, giving your customers more than what they were expecting.

Marketing on Instagram is simple enough. Before you can market your content, you need to first begin by creating your ads. To do this, you need to connect your Instagram account to your *Facebook Business Page* manager. This allows you to use the *Facebook Ad Manager* where you can create ads that run on both Instagram as well on Facebook or just one of the accounts. Facebook owns Instagram's service, so it comes as no surprise that the two services are going to be interconnected.

If you don't have a Facebook account (which could be rare), don't worry too much about it. You can still create a new Instagram account using your email address. However, while you *can* create a new Instagram account without Facebook, *you won't be able to create any ad content <u>without a Facebook</u> account*. If you don't have a Facebook account for your business yet, you need to make one. Once that's done and you've got your profile created, it's time to move onto the next step, which involves the Ad Manager feature.

Ad Manager allows you to build and create ads that you can run on both Instagram and Facebook. Alternatively, you could choose to run it on either platform. Ad Manager is where you go to customize your target audience, make payments, monitor the ad's progress as well as work on other features on the manager. If you already have a Facebook Page, here is how you can connect it to your Facebook Ad Manager:

1. Head to <u>business.facebook.com</u>.

2. Click on **Create Account**.

3. Enter a name for your business, select the primary Page, and enter your name and work email address.

4. Enter all the necessary details requested on the onboarding flow.

Once you are done, link your Instagram account to your Business profile:

1. Go to your Business Manager feature.

2. Click on **Business Settings** located on the left side of the page. Click on it again to **Instagram Accounts**.

3. Click **Claim New Instagram Account**.

4. Add your username and password. When you're done, click **Next**.

5. To authorize one or more of your ad accounts to use the Instagram Account, check the box next to each ad account and click **Save Changes**.

Instagram's advertising works on the same premise as Facebook, utilizing advertising tools.

To get started creating your first ad, follow the steps below:

**Stage #1: Creating Your Content**

Use Facebook's Ad Manager to get started. Once you've selected that option, you will then be directed to the Ad Campaign, Ad Set, and Ad Levels section. This is where you will be able to create multiple ads. These multiple ads can be used to fit into a single ad set, which can then be used to fit under a single ad campaign.

On the *Ad Campaign* feature, choose the objectives for your ad. There is a list of objectives where you can choose from, and these include to build brand awareness, increase traffic and reach, boost engagement, enhance lead generation, prioritize video views or app installs, messages, conversions, catalog sales, and more.

The *Ad Set* feature allows you to choose your target audience, set your budget, decide on your ad placement, and schedule your content and bid. Target your audience based on their job title, language, gender, age, parental status, relationship status, diet, whether they are engaged online shoppers or not, where they shop (high-end or budget retail), and more. These targeting options will be advantageous to you if you're not relying on custom audience advertising.

On the *Ad Level* phase, decide what your creative content should be. This is the phase where you shape what your ad content is going to look like, what it says, and ultimately, determine how successful your ad will be.

## Stage #2: Ad Placement Selection

Facebook's Ad Manager usually already has most of its placements selected automatically. You can opt to change these placements of course, by simply clicking the "Edit" button. With Instagram Ads, you can opt to run other ad placements options simultaneously, even if you're running other ads on your Instagram newsfeed.

## Stage #3: Budget & Schedule

Budgeting is a big consideration for all businesses, both big and small. In terms of budgeting, Instagram offers two options: *a daily or lifetime budget*. The difference between the two options will be discussed below.

## Stage #4: Place Your Bids

Both Facebook and Instagram ads work on a bidding system. What this means is that whoever is willing to bid more will be the one who wins the ad placement for its target audience. Similar to how an auction works. Your bid would depend on what you're optimizing for. For example, what you could be bidding for could include bids for impressions, daily unique reach, landing page views, clicks, and more.

The manual bidding option will give you the most control over how much you're spending per result for your Instagram ads. You have the option of putting a cap on your bid amount, safeguarding yourself against overspending.

**Stage #5: Choosing Your Ad Formats**

Instagram offers four types of formats to choose from - *carousel ads, single ad images, Stories ads, canvas image ads, and video ads.* The single image ads are the most straightforward, simple type of ads there is. Straight to the point, clear, concise, and they work brilliantly for ads which only want to feature single products or something with high visual appeal. You can't go wrong with this ad option.

Carousel ads are also known as multiple ad images. If you're planning to showcase several different products, it gives you more space to elaborate your content and the point that you're trying to make with your audience. Videos can also be slipped into your carousel ad selection to "spice things up" a little and create even more engaging content.

Video ads on Instagram work like Facebook, whereby they run on auto-play. They also start automatically playing without sound, although this is easily fixed by adding closed captions into your videos. The best video ads are kept at 60 seconds or less, and a minimum of 15 seconds at least to start.

**How Do Instagram Ads Work?**

If you haven't started exploring Instagram ads, you should. Instagram has a huge audience growth rate and is among the fastest-growing social media platform to date. At the moment, Instagram offers five ad formats. These are:

1. Photo ads
2. Video Ads
3. Carousel ads
4. Canvas Story Ads
5. Story ads

Instagram Ads work a little differently from Facebook since Instagram this platform relies heavily on images. Unlike Facebook, there's not a lot of texts or wordings involved in the advertising process. Instead, you will be marketing your brand's content through a series of images or videos (or even one image or video), which can be accompanied by a very short text or relevant hashtag. All of these ads options above seamlessly incorporate into the target audience's feeds and stories, enabling a smooth user experience while you browse and explore Instagram. These are integrated with Facebook Ad manager, so marketers have the advantage of utilizing Facebook's user data to enable targeting at a precise level.

One benefit that comes with using Instagram Ads is the granular control which you get to target your audience base with as much specificity as possible. You can target the age, location, gender, interests, and behavior of your viewer base on more, which allows you to create more impactful marketing campaigns which will resonate with your audience. Choose from any of the five campaign options above, depending on what your marketing goals and objectives are.

# Vertical Videos Explained

Social media users are transitioning from news feed ads and unto story ads because of its more vibrant and engaging nature. Frequent users of Instagram know all about the Instagram Stories feature, where users upload an image or a video that is available at the top of their page for a full 24-hours before it disappears. Instagram Story ads exist within this same space as this Story feature. Meaning these ads are going to appear on top of your newsfeed, shot in full-screen vertical video formats and optimized for mobile viewing. Story ads would appear in between the other stories in their newsfeed, sort of like dividers. You've probably experienced this yourself when you're watching a story that a friend uploaded, and before stories move on to *another friend's* story content, a random ad which appears in between.

Vertical videos are the way to go, and the preferred choice among Instagram users for the sake of convenience. Instagrammers prefer not to have to keep turning their mobile phones sideways just to view a video, which is why on Instagram, vertical videos are the ones that work best. The vertical format makes it ideal for mobile viewing on the go; which is how most of the viewership is taking place these days anyway.

## Instagram Stories and Filters

Frequent Instagram users are no stranger to the Stories feature and the cute filters that go along with it. Instagrammers (including businesses) can record a story, add it to their profile highlights and it will remain there for the next 24-hours. Your followers will be able to view your Stories as many times as they like within the next 24-hours before the content vanishes. This is useful for marketing content which is exclusive, such as a one-time offer or a behind-the-scenes sneak peek at what's coming to entice your audience.

Stories were introduced back in August 2016, and it has been growing in popularity ever since. It only took Instagram a year and a half to bring in [300 million users](#) daily, all thanks to the introduction of Instagram Stories. With the introduction of more interactive features (filters, stickers and more) in May 2017, Stories just got even better.

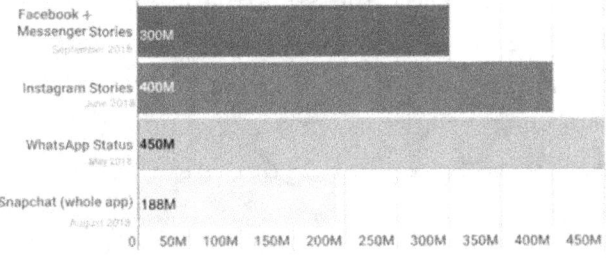

*Source: TechCrunch*

Simple and easy to use, upload any images you've taken on your camera roll within the last 24-hours on to your Instagram Stories.

Instagram Stories comes with the following functions:

- 15-second length videos (max)
- 10-second image views
- Unlimited Stories can be added to your profile
- Viewers can contact you directly and respond to your Stories

Stories are great for marketing purposes because they allow you to cross-promote content across your other social media platforms. Entice viewers to join your contests or special promotions (because of the time-sensitive element of having only 24-hours, they're more inclined to act faster). Get creative with the filters (avoid going overboard though, because you still want to remain consistent with your brand image).

One of the pros of using the Stories feature is that it is great for enticing the younger demographic, and it is growing in popularity right now. The cons are that it is easy to quickly skip over your ad, which means that you run the risk of limited audience engagement.

**IGTV Explained**

50% of businesses on Instagram create at least one Instagram Story ad per month. 81% of businesses use videos as a tool that is part of their overall marketing strategy. 92% of viewers who watch this content on mobile will be keen to share it with others. Those are stats your business can't afford to ignore, and the reason why video has become a necessity for social media marketing.

In 2017, Forbes' Head of Product and Tech, Salah Zalatimo commented in 2017 that vertical videos are going to be the future and the way moving forward for mobile videos, especially when we are already seeing a 15- 25% increase in click-to-play vertical video content. The vertical video trend was made popular by another social media platform - Snapchat - in early 2010. By 2016, SnapChat boasted an impressive 10 billion daily views for their videos. By mid-2016, Instagram was on board with the vertical video trend, launching their IGTV back in June 2018.

Instagram described its IGTV addition as a *"re-envisioned mobile video which has a new standalone surface, a platform which will feature videos longer in length and a platform which is easy to discover through channels, all in one vertical format which fits in the palm of your hand"*. IGTV allows its users to upload longer length videos on this platform, and they won't disappear within 24-hours, like what it's Stories feature does. Users can easily share and view content across this feature. An IGTV channel must be linked to an existing Instagram account. IGTV has its own separate app too, like how Facebook has Facebook Messenger. Two separate apps, two separate platforms, but they can function individually and side by side, complementing each other.

To optimize your IGTV videos, the guidelines below would serve as a rule of thumb you could aim to try and follow for each content:

- Keep your content short (2-5 minutes max).

- Keep your videos at least 1080 x 1920 pixels.

- The orientation of your videos should be vertical (portrait mode).

- Keep your videos at a 4:5 (minimum) and 9:16 (maximum) aspect ratio.

- Minimize the risk of content getting clipped by trying to create a little room around your videos.

- Your video format should be in MP4.

- The size of your video should be capped at 650MB if it is less than 10-minutes long.

- The size of your video should be capped at 3.6GB if your videos go up to about 60 minutes or so.

If you want to keep your videos without posting them on your profile, opt for IGTV instead.

**Instagram Carousel Ads Explained**

Carousel ads allow users to swipe through a series of videos or images. Like a carousel, your content moves one after the other with each swipe. Creative marketers will love this feature, because it provides a creative space to tell a longer story to their audience, allowing them to highlight multiple products, share different perspectives or dive into a single service in a combination of videos or images.

If you want to show the versatility of your content or to show various creative assets such as fashion, food, and design. This feature works great for exercise and fitness profiles, recipe and food profiles, and even makeup and travel. Like the other ads, carousel ads can also be targeted to a certain segment, and a call-to-action button connects your viewers directly from the ad and to your website where they can make their purchases.

**Canvas Story Ads Explained**

Facebook Canvas is another immersive video format ad for Instagram Stories specifically optimized for mobile use. It loads quickly for a smoother viewing experience. On Facebook, there are plenty of Canvas templates that make it easy for you to build a Canvas ad that suits your needs for Instagram. Choose one of these ad templates or build their own custom Canvas for a unique ad experience. These templates enable you to use a combination of videos and photos to showcase variety. These templates are great if you want to show a variety of products and include a campaign video.

**How Much Do These Ads Cost?**

The cost of Instagram Ads would vary depending on several factors. One way in which price points are determined is on the cost-per-click and cost-per-impressions. Another factor that determines cost would be Instagram's ad auction, while other factors which could influence how much you will be paying for your ad include your audience and the ad feedback which you receive.

Determining the actual cost of Instagram ads can be tricky, but you'll be glad to know that you can control how your marketing budget will be allocated for these ads. For example, you have the option of choosing a daily budget limit (which is the amount you're willing to spend per day), or a lifetime budget (which is where you can select your ads to be advertised for a period of time until your budget has reached its capacity). You will also be able to control your ad expenses by selecting the ad schedule you prefer, the delivery method of your ad, and the bid amount you prefer.

A lifetime budget could prove to be your best bet if you are keen on letting Facebook automatically distribute your ad spend for you for a fixed amount of time. With this option, there's one guarantee which you get - you will never be over your advertising budget if you happen to schedule incorrectly for example.

**Creating Content That Goes Viral**

That depends on the mathematical calculations and a little bit of luck. Instagram uses its own algorithm to determine which posts it is going to select to appear at the top. Getting on Instagram's Explore section (available through the "search" feature on the app) is the best way to quickly boost your brand's image and get a much wider viewership.

When Lady Luck is on your side, your content could go viral within an hour. If you don't want to rely entirely on luck alone, the suggestions below are some you should keep in mind to create content Instagrammers won't be able to resist:

- Use the right hashtags.

- Have a call-to-action in your caption to enhance engagement.

- Create or curate content which is going to have the most potential to appeal to your audience. It's okay to post content which has already gone viral if it's something you think your audience is going to enjoy.

- Stick to a theme which is consistent with your audience demographic.

- Post at a time when your audience is the most active.

# Chapter 3: #GrowYourFollowing

Instagram. It's every marketer's best friend. The potential for greater advertising on Instagram is better than ever, and by the looks of it, things are only going to get better as newer and better features keep getting rolled out. Social media is so easy to use that everyone could do it, and because it's free to join, it's the most accessible platform readily available to anyone with a smart device and a good internet connection.

Instagram has become such an indispensable marketing tool because it is among the simplest and most effective ways of reaching your target audience. Effective marketing, though, is more than just being able to post a pretty photo on your business profile. It takes careful planning, focus, and the help of several tools to truly make your advertising efforts a success. Running a successful Instagram ad or marketing campaign can sometimes be a hit or miss process, but the availability of certain tools that could enhance your marketing efforts, you could tip the scales in your favor towards success. All you need to do is start tapping into these tools for maximum advantage.

## Basic Third-Party Instagram Tools You Need for Consistent Content

Instagram tools are here to make your life easier. You're going to have a lot on your plate, what with managing your business and steering it in the direction you want to go without compromising other areas of your life to do it. From sourcing products to dealing with customers, business owners have their hands full, and if there are tools available to help you manage your workload, why not make full use of them?

The social media world is a competitive one. You must stay ahead if you want to stay in the game, but at times, staying one step ahead seems nearly impossible when you're busy being pulled in all sorts of directions. What can you do to ensure you never miss a content post or always respond in a prompt and timely manner? By relying on the Instagram-related tools that are readily available online.

Instagram does provide some good options within its platform to help you maximize your content, but these third-party tools are there to make it *even better*. Some of these tools aren't just Instagram specific either, so there's the advantage of using them across your other social media platforms. These tools are to suit a variety of purposes, but each just as useful as the next at helping you put your best marketing efforts forward.

## *Third-Party Content Scheduling Tools*

Posting consistently at the same time each day is going to be an impossible goal to accomplish. You *may want to,* but at the last minute, things could come up. You might get distracted and forget. Or you could miss your ideal schedule time and miss an opportunity while you're at it. Either way, it's risky to do it manually, and these third-party scheduling tools are here to provide a solution.

- **Tool #1: Hootsuite** - A useful tool for both scheduling your content, and monitoring how it's going. Schedule your content ahead of time and get notified so you can keep track of it quickly and easily. As a web-based platform, Hootsuite allows you to manage multiple social media accounts, not just Instagram alone.

- **Tool #2: Schedugram** - The perfect option for scheduling all types of posts, although it is one of the more pricier tools compared to a lot of the other ones mentioned. Schedugram comes with features which include content creation, a feature which is explicitly designed for Instagram. Its built-in photo editing, location, shopping, drag and drop calendar function, mention, carousel ad options, videos, and stories are only a peek into what this tool is capable of.

- **Tool #3: Buffer** - Perfect for scheduling content, and it comes with both a free and pro version (which is paid for). This tool allows users to schedule single-image posts right from their desktops or mobile apps, conveniently allowing you to schedule ahead of time.

## *Third-Party Multiple Account Managing Tools*

Managing multiple social media platforms can be challenging and time-consuming. But a business today isn't going to have just one social media platform alone. Which is why these multichannel tools are going to be a lifesaver during these moments:

- **Tool #1: CrowdFire** - Run on a web-based platform, this "everything under one roof" social media management tool lets you control your blog content, schedule, publish, curate, and even track your social media mentions all through this one, seamless tool. With both free and paid options available, this social media account management tool is perfect for the busy marketer who's got a lot on their plate. Need to monitor your post analytics and social media accounts (not just Instagram)? CrowdFire can do that for you, too.

- **Tool #2: Status Rew** - A tool that is perfect if you've got 10 social media profiles, 10 Twitter sources, 2000 scheduled posts per profile, and three members running the show. Status Rew includes social listening features too, which means you can sync your social engagement to the platform, draft replies, monitor keywords, and even moderate comments without ever having to switch back and forth between Instagram and this tool. Talk about a time-saver!

- **Tool #3: Sendible** - This tool has got Canva integration, plus team collaborations features, CRM, and account and social media management which make scheduling and managing your Instagram account a breeze. The only catch is that it can be a little on the pricier side. This is because it is designed mostly for agencies. Small business owners and those who are just starting out might find the added monthly cost with this one a pinch on the budget, but it does come with some really great, robust features if you're willing to spend some money.

## *Third-Party Content Creation Tools*

You've got a lot of great ideas for content on your Instagram account, but sometimes, you might need a hand bringing these great ideas to life. That's where these content creation tools come in, to help you turn your ideas into reality, only better:

- **Tool #1: Canva** - From email headers to Instagram posts, Canva will leave you spoilt for choice when it comes to which templates to use for your Instagram profile. This tool comes with both free and paid templates for you to choose from to help you create your best content yet. You can even choose to upload your finished products directly onto your Instagram account once you're happy with it.

- **Tool #2: Report** - Reposting can be a big help to your marketing efforts, especially when it comes to encouraging user-generated content. This free tool offers the option of both sharing and curating content to take some of the stress of creating good content away. With Repost, your favorite videos and photos on Instagram can quickly and easily be reposted, but remember to give credit to the original owner of the content though if you're reposting anything from a follower or influencer.

- **Tool #3: Boomerang** - Those quirky, funny, short video loops you've become so accustomed to on Instagram are hard to miss. Who doesn't love to be entertained by a good Boomerang? It was a stand-alone app, but now, it is built-in as part of Instagram's story features, and it is absolutely perfect for creating on-the-go short video loops anytime, anywhere.

### *Third-Party Photo Editing Tools*

Not every filter is going to do your picture or video justice. Sometimes, you need to bring in the big guns for even better, more professional looking content. Content that is so well-edited your customers can't help but notice. Remember, Instagram relies heavily on visuals. The better your content is, the more stopping-power it is going to have.

- **Tool #1: Photoshop Express** - Good old Photoshop. It's always there to save the day. A longtime favorite, Photoshop Express has a wide array of features to help take your images one step further. Anything from cropping, text tools, exposure corrections, perspective corrections, blemish removal, filters, and border additions, this tool is here to satisfy all your photo editing needs.

- **Tool #2: Afterlight 2** - The array of choices help you pick the best ones that will make an impact on your images. An all-in-one tool for all your photo editing needs, Afterlight 2 can quickly become a favorite because of all the filters, frames, and typography options that it presents you with. You even have the option of creating your own filters with this one.

- **Tool #3: Facetune** - If you're not keen on fancy editing programs like Photoshop, this one might do the trick, although it is more suitable for photos with apparel products. For the images that need a little help and touching up, give Facetune a go.

## *Third-Party Hashtag Tools*

A good hashtag is going to make or break your content. It can mean the difference between whether your content goes viral (along with the hashtag), or gets lost in Instagram's vast sea of existing content. Without a hashtag, your post might look almost naked and incomplete on your profile. How do you source the most suitable hashtags for your content? Aside from targeting those with the highest number of uses, these third-party tools are here to help you determine which hashtags you should be using:

- **Tool #1: AutoHash** - Autohash will review the images on your profile, detect the objects within that image, and then proceed to suggest which hashtags might be the most relevant to your content using artificial intelligence. You can sign up for free, but any extras would come with in-app purchases for additional features. This is an Android-based app though, and it will help you locate the relevant hashtags on Instagram for your business.

- **Tool #2: TopTager** - This is quickly becoming every marketer's best go-to, because not only does it display all the most popular and trending hashtags in real-time, it also helps locate the hashtags which will be the best match for your keywords.

- **Tool #3: Focal Mark** - For an app that works on both iOS and Android, Focal Mark chooses which hashtags are going to work best for your profile. It uses an algorithm which takes the photo's subject, location, and the camera which was used to capture that content. It then helps you detect the most popular hashtags which would be the most relevant to your content.

**Locating Your Influencers**

Prominent Instagrammers are known as influencers, and they usually command a large number of followers and have spent a significant amount of time and effort building up a reputable presence on social media. It is common these days to find businesses working together with influencers and enlisting their help with product endorsement and promotion. Influencers could either be celebrities or if they aren't, they're users with a massive following who have established a name for themselves.

Influencers are everywhere on social media, and eventually, you're going to need to work with them, at least once. But one of the biggest challenges of running a successful marketing campaign is finding the right kind of influencers to work with. The influencer that you choose should be relevant to what your brand represents. They should also have a significant reach, one that is strong enough to help you achieve the advertising campaign goals which you already set forth for yourself before you even began the campaign. Influencer marketing is so successful that some brands even fork out big bucks on celebrity endorsements especially because they see those endorsements as a return on investment. Celebrities like Kylie Jenner can command millions per sponsored post, because of the vast reach and influence that she has.

To source influencers that you could work with, you could start with these two third-party tools:

- **Tool #1: FameBit** - Connect directly with influencers who are on the lookout for new campaign opportunities. Once you've set up your campaign type on this tool (narrowing down your factors and budget), you'll be able to get to work quickly connecting with influencers who are going to be the right fit for what you need.

- **Tool #2: UserGems** - Perfect for helping you locate both influencers and micro-influencers. UserGem uses real-time customer intelligence and data from your customers to help you detect the best influencers who are popular among your niche market. Did you know that these could already exist among your very own existing customer base! Do a quick search and see what you come up with.

**Marketing with Instagram Live**

All businesses want the opportunity to forge more intimate connections, and share genuine experiences with their customers as they are happening. Businesses are no longer a cold, distant, entity that customers have no chance of coming into contact with, because social media, of course, has changed all of that. Customers today can connect with businesses and reach out to them like they would with any of their other friends on social media. They even have the option of doing it *live,* when a business goes on Instagram Live, of course.

For businesses, Instagram can be a great channel for building trust among your audiences. You've probably used this feature a few times on your personal account, sharing live events as they happen because you want your friends and family to share at the moment with you. It works the same way with your business content. This is how you draw new customers into your fold, by being easily accessible and reachable. Instagram Live gives your brand a boost in its discoverability on the platform.

In case you're not familiar with this feature, Live works like every other existing feature on Instagram. Live broadcasts become even more effective if you promote what's coming to build up the anticipation among your audience. If you generate a lot of engagement and views on your content, you'll end up right on the Explore Page for even more audiences to see.

Going Live on Instagram puts you in front and center of your audience. Think of it as if you were going on stage and the spotlight is on you, because that is how it works, even though technically, you're not face-to-face with your audience. But they will be watching you closely, that much you can be sure of. Once your brand goes live, you will be appearing right at the front of their Stories feed, which guarantees that they are bound to take notice if they're on Instagram. Some customers might have even adjusted their settings to receive notifications once anyone they follow starts a Live video broadcast.

## Choosing Your "Live" Content

Before you can begin to run your marketing campaign on Live, you need to decide *what type* of campaign you're going for. Among the more popular campaign options used by existing businesses on Instagram include:

- **Product Release Campaigns** - The grand unveiling of products and new releases is given a more dramatic impact when the announcement comes in the form of an Instagram Live video. There are so many possibilities to work with this feature, ranging from special Q&A sessions with the designers of the product, honest testimonial sessions from longtime customers, even a Live discussion with the team who was responsible for creating that product and what inspired them to do so.

- **Live Event Campaigns** - Sometimes, the best approach is the simplest approach. For special occasions and events that you think your customers would enjoy, a Live event is a way to go. This could be events which you're either attending or hosting, anything that is exciting which you would like to share with your followers. If it is an event which you are organizing for your customers, broadcast it so those who couldn't be there on that day still get to be part of the action and watch what's happening.

- **Instructional Guide Campaigns** - Prior to a big launch, part of your marketing plan could be to launch a series of instructional videos and how-to campaigns you think your customer might benefit from. These campaigns always resonate well with audiences, because you can bet that they will have a ton of questions about your product. This type of campaign works really well for skincare lines in particular.

- **Sneak Peak Campaigns -** A sneak peek at new products that are coming is always a very exciting prospect, especially for customers. Instagram Live is great for unveiling your latest range of products, maybe even to tease your audiences by giving them a sneak preview before the actual launch. Don't forget to include call-to-actions or links which direct your audiences where to go and how to make a purchase.

## How to Create Quality Content Your Audience Wants

Your business should have *one aim* when it comes to social media platforms like Instagram. *Make an impression.* Be remembered and set yourself apart from your competitors in every possible way. You want your business to leave its mark among the millions of Instagrammers out there on the platform in the hopes of making more sales. To be that one brand that stands out, you need to create mind-blowing content that is going to make your customers sit up and take notice. *You need to create quality content that they want to see.*

Instagram is a social media platform unlike any other. No other visual-heavy platform has been able to match Instagram just yet in terms of image and video quality and expectations. It may stand out in many ways, but there is *one way* in which Instagram is like the other social media platforms. *Competitiveness*. Make no mistake that the Instagram world is a competitive one. You're vying for the attention of millions of users, competing with thousands, if not millions, of businesses who are *also competing* for the viewers' attention and trying to make them a loyal customer.

Creating quality content doesn't have to be a stressful process when you follow the guidelines below:

- **Going Text-Free** - It's all about the visuals on Instagram, and text comes second to that. While the use of closed captions makes your video easier and much clearer, you should still refrain from putting too much text on your video screen at any given time. The best way to determine you're not doing that is to check your thumbnail videos on Instagram. If you notice that more than 20% of your thumbnail image is being overshadowed by text, you'll know it's far too much.

- **Make Time to Curate Before It's Too Late** - Don't let the stress and pressure of having to post content consistently, daily, and even several times a day get to you. *Definitely, don't* post content for the sake of being active on social media. The best strategy that you can employ for your business is to spend time collecting, refining, and curating your content to ensure that only the best gets shared with your audience. This way, you *know you're* giving your audience what you believe they want to see.

- **Solve A Problem** - What customers want to see is a solution to their problem. If you can offer them that in each content you post, they'll be eager to come back for more. By helping them identify and solve a problem, you're in effect creating a bond with them and forging a connection. Problem-solving content shows the audience that your brand understands and more importantly, cares about what they're going through.

- **Run A Contest** - Instagram contests are enticing for audiences, especially if they have been loyal followers of your brand and product. That build-up of anticipation creates the much-needed buzz that will put your product in the spotlight. They'll be eager to participate in the hopes of winning, which is why contests are a brilliant way to boost engagement for a new product that you may be launching soon.

- **Tell Them Your Story -** A business that shows its customers its human side through the content it shares is the one that wins them over. Your customers love to know what's the inspiration behind your company. What drives you as a brand each morning to get up and seize the day? This is one of the reasons why they are following you in the first place. They want to see your passion, your dedication, and your commitment and build that human connection that makes you more than just another brand to your customers.

- **Tell Others *Their* Story -** Without your customers, your business wouldn't be what it is today. Show them some love by sharing their inspirational stories on your account for other users to see (with their permission, of course). Let your customers feel involved in your community. Make them feel that your brand cares about them. That's the kind of content that other users want to see.

## Important Design Reminders to Create Great Content

Snap, shoot, record, and upload might work for regular Instagram users who are simply sharing their daily activities for thoughts, but brands and business work on an entirely different level. For a brand, simply snapping and shooting without a purpose is how you're going to lose followers. *Every single piece of content* you produce and that gets displayed on your social media account must have a clear point of focus. If you observe the most successful Instagram marketing campaigns online, you'll notice that a common design theme which emerges is that the content has a focal point. There may be several objects within one picture, but always *just one* that stands out. That's the focal point.

You need to design your content around a clear focal point. This should be the object or product that you want your audience to zoom in on. The only one they should notice aside from the colorful background and catchy captions. A clear focal point means that your audience's eye needs to be immediately drawn to the primary subject of your image composition.

When you're work on creating content your audience wants to see, ***follow the rule of thirds*** for the design aspect. It's a classic photography rule, and every professional photography knows the rule of thirds like the back of their hand.

With this rule, you need to imagine that your image is made up of a 9-part grid overlaying that image. Mentally divide your image into two vertical and two horizontal lines running across the square box. Now, once you've imagined that, you need to then align your most interesting features along the grid's intersections. To create the perfect shot, the focal point of your content should be about one-third of that image. The idea behind this concept is that the off-center composition which you will end up with is a lot more pleasing to the audience's eye because it appears more natural. It also encourages you to use the negative space or empty areas around your focal point creatively.

You also want to pay attention to the balance and contrast of your content. Making your image stand out from the crowd is entirely up to you, and how well you're able to balance and contrast your image composition to create the perfect result you desire. Contrasting elements are key to helping your Instagram image stand out in the news feed. Contrasting elements here can refer to several different things, including light, exposure, color, shapes, scale, fonts, and more.

Finally, it's okay if you don't fill your entire image box from end to end. There's nothing wrong with having white borders around your images. In fact, an image with a border on Instagram has the potential to create an unusual effect which could end up attracting your audience even more. This helps to ensure that your image's design elements have some breathing room, so you don't risk accidentally cropping anything off.

# Chapter 4: Insightful Advice

Without insight into how your marketing campaign is going, you'll be navigating your campaign blindfolded, shooting in the dark, and hoping you'll get a successful hit out of it. It's easy to forget about insights when you're caught up in running your campaign, planning your content, and trying to make sure you're bringing in as many new customers as possible. *But you need insights.* You need the vital information it provides you with that tells you whether your marketing campaign is on the right track or not. Otherwise, you could be spending all your efforts on futile attempts that yield very little results.

Time is precious in business and every second count. The last thing you want is to reach the end of your campaign timeframe and realize you didn't achieve a single goal or target you set out to do. Since these campaigns cost money, you quite *literally* cannot afford any mistakes which can be avoided, like skipping out on Instagram Insights.

## Instagram Insights and How It Works

A native analytics tool on Instagram's platform, Insights provides marketers with the data that they need about their follower demographics. This includes details about who your followers are, any action they have taken on your content, and it lets you know which content on your account is doing well. This is all crucial information that you need as a marketer to measure the success and performance of each campaign you run. You need to keep tabs on what's working and what isn't.

Insights are available to anyone with an Instagram business account. You will be able to access this feature immediately as soon as you've set up your business profile. You can't view this if your profile remains personal. To access Insights directly from your profile page, what you would need to do is look at the upper-right hand corner of your mobile phone screen, and then tap the bar graph icon at the top.

*Image Source: HubSpot*

The main Insights home page will provide you with a summary overview of the data from the content which you have posted over the past seven days. You will be able to view details such as how many followers you have gained over the past seven days and how much engagement you received per post during that same period.

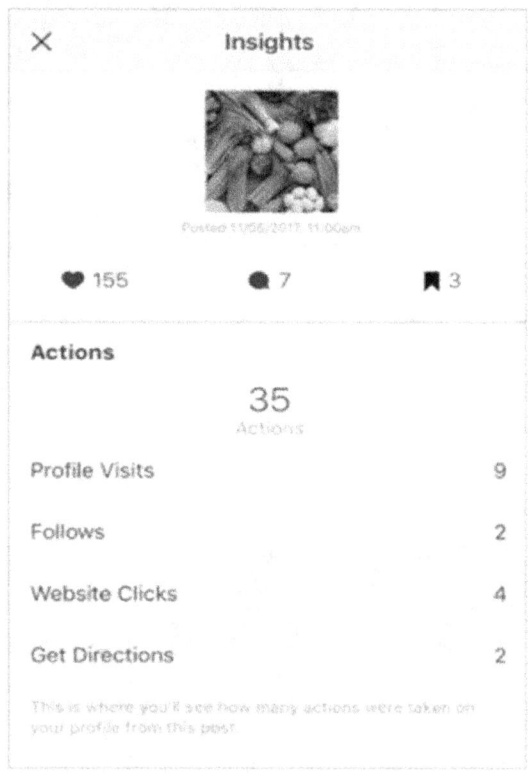

*Image Source: HubSpot*

With insights, you gain access to information regarding:

- The gender and age group of your followers.

- Their online behavior patterns and trends.

- Where your followers are based.

- The number of profile views and clicks.

- How often they are online daily.

- How much engagement you're receiving on your profile.

- How to filter your content based on metrics, content type, and timeframe.

- How much impressions each post received and the ratio of reach and engagement per post.

- How many users have started following your profile.

- How many times users have swiped away at your Story to skip it.

- How many times users have clicked on the links included in your business profile.

- What your best and worst-performing content was.

- Data related to your Instagram Stories metrics.

All the information that you gather from here will help you plan and prepare better for the next few steps you need to take. Without insights, it's going to be difficult to execute any effective strategies to begin marketing your business.

**Setting Your Marketing Goals**

Before the strategies come the goal-setting portion of the plan. With the percentage of users growing every year, Instagram advertising is poised to take over the world. Businesses are quickly falling in love with this social media site (if they aren't already) because of the endless new possibilities that have been made possible, especially when it comes to connecting with their customers. Businesses have been able to dramatically connect with their audiences, engage with their target demographics, and drive sales like never before, all thanks to the power of social media.

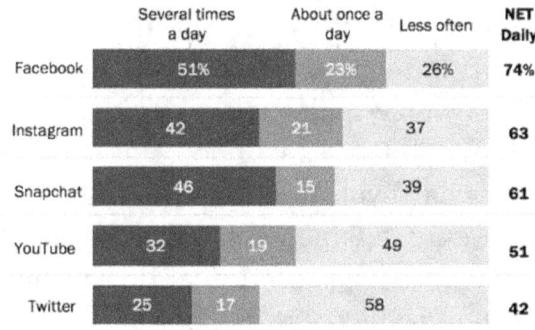

*Image Source: <u>Brand Watch</u>*

Since the social media space is extremely competitive, a business has its work cut out for it when it comes to successfully marketing themselves well enough to stand out. For a brand to call its advertising efforts successful, it must develop a well-defined, creative, and detailed advertising strategy. This can only be done if a brand has a clearly defined set of advertising goals which can produce measurable results. Before you begin, you need to define your goals.

## *Business Goals - What They Are and Why You Need Them*

Defining your business and marketing goals is not easy. In fact, it is one of the many hard aspects of running a successful business. Without the right strategy and goals to guide you down the path, your business will be going nowhere no matter how hard you think you're trying to make it work. Many businesses (old and new) still struggle with this aspect. A goal doesn't mean *"I want as many followers as possible"*. That's not definitive enough. Every goal you set must be as specific as possible, down to the very last and smallest details. The more detail you have, the better your marketing and advertising strategy will be.

To define your goals, you're going to have to work on two phases. *Phase 1* is where you need to first address the following questions (in detail, of course):

- What does success mean to you?

- What are you primarily using this platform for? (Better connect with your target demographic? Build greater brand awareness? Develop brand loyalty?)

- What type of content are you planning to market on Instagram?

- Why did you choose Instagram for your business?

- How do you believe Instagram will help you achieve your marketing goals?

- How much financially can you commit to your advertising budget?

- How much time can you commit to advertising daily on Instagram?

- How is Instagram different from your other social media platforms?

The advertising goals which you set will have a heavy influence on the kind of metrics which you will use to track the success of your efforts. There could be a long list of reasons and rationales for using Instagram and why you think this method of advertising is going to best help your business meet its goals. But if you can clearly define each reason in detail, you're off to a good start.

Now, for *Phase 2*, the start of the goal-setting process. In *Phase 2*, this is what you need to address *before* ultimately defining your final goals:

- **Step 1: Defining Your Business Objectives.** Ideally, your objectives should try to increase brand awareness among your target audience. The most important question you should ask is *what* does your business hope to achieve by advertising on Instagram? What can you do on Instagram that you cannot with other social media platforms? Your objectives could include seeking to build a community with better engagement, connect your brand with both audiences and influencers, and increase sales by driving traffic to your site. It depends on what you want to Instagram to help you achieve for your business.

- **Step 2: Defining Who Your Audience Is.** Who are you targeting specifically? What are the details of this demographic? A helpful approach here would be customer profiling, which gives you a better sense of the type of content your target customer is after. What hashtags do they use? What communities are they are involved in on Instagram? Think of this stage as your due diligence. The more information you can gather to create your customer persona, the more definitive your advertising strategy will be.

Being as definitive as possible every step of the way is going to make things a lot easier on both you and the team of people working in your company. Your staff could benefit from being clear about what their responsibilities are to ensure that everyone is doing what they're supposed to and working towards the goal.

As your business changes and grows, your goals are going to shift and change right along with the needs of your business. Once you've accomplished one goal, it's not uncommon for another to quickly take its place. The key to successful advertising on Instagram is learning how to identify which goals will be complemented by the right kind of advertising objectives.

**Effective Strategies to Start Marketing Your Business**

Many businesses are often left bewildered, wondering *why* their marketing efforts did not work quite as well as they hoped. What they don't realize is that having the right growth strategies is the missing link and that link is something not a lot of marketers are aware of. To create content that is going to hit every business goal and target you set, it must be accompanied by the right marketing strategies if you hope to avoid wasting a lot of time, energy, and resources on measures that are not doing anything to help boost your business sales.

Effective marketing strategies that are going to help you market and grow your business should be the foundation on which your campaign is built. To achieve that outcome, the following marketing strategies need to be your core focus:

### *Effective Strategy #1: Plan Ahead*

Napoleon Hill once said, *plan your work and work your plan*. Running a successful business is a major undertaking, and effective strategies require thought, careful consideration, fine-tuning, and preparation. The best way to prepare yourself for this challenge is to plan ahead as much as possible. Ideally, you want to aim to try and plan for your content at least two to three weeks in advance. This gives you enough time to work on perfecting it before it gets published. If what you are doing is snapping a picture on that day and uploading it 5 minutes later, that is not going to be very effective at driving the growth of your business.

## *Effective Strategy #2: Don't Skimp Out on Research*

No content can be executed well without proper planning and preparation as a foundation. Never skip the due diligence part of the process, you'll be glad that you didn't. Even if your business is small, never underestimate the power of what research could do for your business plan. Do your research until you have got a good idea about where the future of your industry is headed, and what you can do to stay ahead of the competitive game. Do your research until you understand the industry that you are in as a whole. Do your research until you are familiar with what kind of competitive landscape you are dealing with. Do your research and find out what your competitors are doing, and whether it's working or not. If it is working, why? What are they doing right that you need to start doing? What can you learn from your competitor's campaigns that were not as successful? All the answers that you seek will be within your research findings.

## *Effective Strategy #3: Curate to Perfection*

The best strategy that you can employ for your business is to spend time collecting, refining, and curating your content to ensure that only the best gets shared with your audience. Perfection here is trying to make your content the best that it can be *without* striving for unrealistic expectations. Content curation has been mentioned a couple of times, and it's being mentioned again because your content reflects everything that your business stands for. More importantly, it needs to be something that inspires them to want to act, specifically, to buy the products you're trying to sell. That is how you encourage and motivate them, and hopefully, translate that into a boost in your sales numbers.

## *Effective Strategy #4: Timing Is Everything*

The right time, the right post. Timing is everything, and a big part of ensuring that your content is effective is to post it at the right time when it is likely to be seen by the largest number of audiences. Go back to your Instagram Analytics, and observe over several weeks when your audiences are the most active online. Once you have got a gauge of when the right time to post should be, you need to experiment. Try posting during these times and see if your engagement levels increased compared to when you posted content at various other timings.

## *Effective Strategy #5: Formulating A Hashtag Library*

To maximize both your time and efficiency, create a library of hashtags that you use on your content. Instead of spending time thinking about which hashtag you should put up next, or scrolling through old content trying to find the best hashtags that worked in the past, stay one step ahead by creating a list or library of your most popular hashtags. Refer to content that has done extremely well in the past, or received the highest number of engagements, that should give you an idea. Having quick access to this list is going to save you a lot of time while simultaneously ensuring that the right hashtags always get published for maximum results.

The survival of your business will depend on how effective your growth strategies are. Part of running a business is having to make a lot of critical decisions, sometimes, on the spot. This means that you must allocate all your resources wisely, especially when it comes to marketing and advertising. Instagram is a global phenomenon, which means that there will be millions of other brands competing and vying for the same attention from your audience just like what you are doing. To come out on top you must be able to increase your chances of making yourself heard loud and clear. The final piece of advice? Be professional at all times. It may be a social media profile, but professionalism still matters in everything that you do.

**Managing Your Ads**

Managing a successful Instagram marketing campaign is a lot of work. Sometimes, it can even seem overwhelming when you think about everything that needs to be done. With so much information to filter and sift through, how do you know what's going to work best and what isn't? For the ads in your marketing campaign to be considered a success, they must reach the right audience. After all, that's the whole point, isn't it? To draw in new customers while you simultaneously retain the existing ones you have by keeping them interested.

Most businesses would have at least two social media accounts that they run, one of which is Facebook. Now, since Facebook and Instagram work on a similar premise almost, this makes it easier for you to track, run, and set up campaigns on your Instagram account in the same way you would for Facebook. Meaning you don't have to double your workload doing two separate campaigns. Moreover, since Instagram uses the same advertising tools that Facebook does, if you know what to do on one platform, the other is going to be a piece of cake.

The easiest way to keep track of and manage your ads is through the Ads Manager function. The dashboard has everything that you need, especially at a quick glance. The data that you'll be presented with includes what your cost per action is, how much results you're getting, relevance score, and more. Monitoring your ad campaigns closely will help you see what's working, what's not, pull the plug on ineffective ad campaigns, and determine how you can reallocate your ad spend budget on more successful ones. Keep a close eye on your campaigns by checking in on them regularly. The system can seem intimidating at first when you're still trying to figure it all out, but the beauty of social media is that it's so easy to use, you'll pick it up in no time.

Since you're going to be managing more than one ad at a time, a great tip to boost engagement is by boosting your content. Instagram also has a *Boost Post* option, you will only be paying to promote one specific post (so make it your best one!). Any business account can take full advantage of this feature and boost any content that you like. To access this option, go to your Instagram business profile and select a post; here you will be able to see the option "Promote", which should be placed directly below the image. Clicking on this option will prompt you to select your focus objective, and you will only have two options to choose from. The first option could be to increase your website and profile visits, and the second option is to reach your target audience based on their location. When you have selected the objective of your choosing, you will then be prompted to choose your call to action, determine how long you want to run your campaign, and set your budget. Be sure to preview your ad before you submit it though.

**Keeping Track of Your Success**

Managing social media marketing campaigns is going to require a lot of investment on your part, in terms of time and money. You *need* to know if your efforts have paid off and whether each campaign is as successful as you hoped it would be. Did you meet all your marketing goals? The only way to gauge your success is to track it.

The metrics and tools provided by a lot of these social media platforms certainly make the life of a marketer a lot easier. It would be extremely tedious to manually track each detail otherwise. Measure the success of your marketing campaigns against the following benchmarks:

- **Comment Numbers** - How many comments are you getting on your content? Is that number rising or declining? This metric can be a telling indicator of how engaging your Instagram content is. If you barely receive any comments on your content or the number of comments you've been receiving lately is on the decline, that could be an indication that your audience isn't connecting as well with your content as you hoped. Comments are a much stronger indicator than likes are because it takes a lot more time and effort to write a thoughtful comment on content than it does to like it. When your audience takes the time to comment on your content, that means it resonated and spoke to them. They connected with it enough to want to leave a remark, whether positive or negative. At least it evoked some form of emotion with them, and that's what you want to aim for. Producing content which sparks an emotion or reaction.

- **Follower Numbers** - Like the comments, you want to watch for whether your follower numbers have increased or gone south. Organic followers are the only ones that matter, and you should never be tempted to "buy" your followers; that's not a genuine reflection of how well you're doing. Big following numbers always mean that you're doing something right. That your campaign is working the way that you hoped it would. It is equally important to track how impactful your content is on these followers. Switching your focus from how many people are following you to how much *reach* your content is getting is a lot more valuable. Having a bigger reach means your audience is engaged with the content that you're providing. Which is a good thing, since you don't want them to be just aimlessly scrolling through your content with no action.

- **Engagement Per Follower Ratio -** To determine which content is making an impact and resonating with your audience, turn to your engagement per follower ratio. Engagement rates can be calculated on a weekly or even a monthly basis, depending on how often you are posting content on your profile. Keep a lookout for the average number of likes that you're getting per post. Keep tabs on the comments that you receive too and activities such as how many people are visiting your profile and clicking on your website.

- **Referral Numbers** - Looking for an indication about how much traffic your website is getting from your Instagram profile? Check your referral numbers to track your return on investments (ROI). It is entirely possible to track your social media's ROI, and in fact, that is what you *should* be doing to keep tabs on just how successful your marketing campaigns are. Instagram posed a challenge for marketers when it came to tracking ROI because of how the app does not allow your clickable links to be included within posts. To combat that setback, marketers had to turn to UTM parameters to do the trick. UTM parameters are the tags which you add onto a URL. These tags will then give Google Analytics more information about the link. Adding these UTM parameters to the links that your brand shares on Instagram will enable you to accurately track your campaigns and determine which traffic is coming as a direct result of your Instagram content.

- **Hashtag Performance** - Hashtags and Instagram are inseparable. You can't have one without the other; they go together like a pair of twins. Hashtags help to bring in more engagement and make your posts more discoverable. You can even use hashtags to track which ones are getting you the most engagement for your post. Instagram is one of the few platforms out there which encourage the use of multiple hashtags, although you still shouldn't use too many. Remember that hashtag library you started? Well, that's going to be useful for you here. Keeping track of your hashtags and putting together a list of which ones generally draw in the most likes when you use them will help you determine your most effective hashtags. These are going to be the ones that you want to start using most often since they bring in the most traffic. Keeping tabs on hashtags which perform well will also give you a much better idea about what type of content you should be focusing on, which ones your audience wants to see more of. When it comes to content planning, this is going to be a big help during your brainstorming sessions. If at any time you find your hashtags aren't drawing in a lot of likes, review them and see what needs to be changed.

- **Post-Performance** - The first thing you want to do is look at the performance of your posts. Reviewing the impressions, comments, likes, and reposts is a good way to track and understand how each post on your profile is performing. Once you have the statistics and necessary figures, compare that to the details of another post you have done. Determine which one has performed better and why it did. If your audience numbers are growing, but your content doesn't seem to be making much of an impact despite that growth, that's an indication that something needs to change. These valuable insights can help you create much better content going down the road.

# Chapter 5: Marketing Success Within Your Reach

Powerful marketing campaigns can do wonders to transform the performance of your business. From struggling to make a sale to going viral in a day, anything is possible when your marketing campaigns are powerful enough to leave an impression on your customers. Optimizing your marketing campaigns for Instagram should be the core focus of every campaign you intend to run, and there's a lot of work that goes into creating just one campaign alone.

Time, effort, commitment, and not to mention, the budget that is spent, crafting a campaign to perfection until its ready to launch means you need to make sure all your bases are covered. This isn't as easy as it sounds, though, especially when your ideas and ambitions don't line up with the marketing budget you have to work with. Even with a limited budget, though, it's still possible to create powerful campaigns. A great campaign doesn't necessarily have to be accompanied by a big budget all the time. It is still possible to do when you know how to work Instagram's advertising tools to your advantage.

**How to Create Powerful Campaigns**

Creating powerful ad campaigns without having to break the bank requires careful planning and strategy. Plan your most powerful campaign using the guidelines below as a reference:

- **Step 1: Start with Your BEST Objective** - Your objectives list would probably have a few items on it, and it can be hard to narrow it down to just one. Every objective feels like it matters (and it does), but a powerful campaign requires focus. To do that, you need to pick the BEST objective out of that list and focus on that. Otherwise, you're going to end up with an ad that is trying to do too much at once, and at the end of the day, it ends up not being very effective at all. It is always trial and error though when you're attempting to set up new ads, especially in the beginning, so don't get too frustrated and allow yourself some time to adjust to the process and get the feel of how things work best.

- **Step 2: Every Campaign Has a Name** - Every campaign you plan should have its own name. Naming your ad is like a tracking system which is going to keep you organized, and it helps you keep track of what works and what did not. You can pick your campaign names based on campaign type, country, network, demographics, language, and basically anything that you'd like. That way, when you need to refer to a successful past campaign while planning your future ones, recollection is a lot easier and more detailed when you can quickly refer to *Campaign A* instead of trying to randomly recall bits and pieces.

- **Step 3: Deciding on Your Ad Placements** - Instagram's Ad Manager feature provides you with a few ad placement options to choose from. You want to familiarize yourself with their options *before* you start selecting your target audience because it is going to help you decide if this ad is going to actually work well on Instagram, or if it would be best on another social media platform altogether. Ad placements must be edited according to the social media platform because it allows you to better track the performance of the ad. Your Instagram ad campaign should be optimized for the ad specific to the platform, avoid using a standardized format across all your social media profiles. A placement which works well on Instagram might not perform as well on Facebook or Twitter, for example, and vice versa.

- **Step 4: Zone in On Your Audience -** Save yourself a lot of time and money by targeting the right audience group from the very beginning. Your target audience is going to be the tipping point of your campaign, the one that determines if it is a success or failure. To fine-tune your audience reach, select them based on age, gender, location, language, demographics, behavior, and connections to name just a few. By zooming in on the details and fine-tuning your reach, you'll save yourself from spending precious dollars out of your already limited budget targeting the wrong group of customers who aren't going to yield any tangible results. Once you have selected the right audience group for your ad, you'll see the option of "Audience Definition" on your ads manager display. Use this function, because it is going to tell you if you have targeted your audience too broadly or too specifically.

- **Step 5: Customize Your Budget** - The great thing about Instagram is the flexibility it offers when you need it. Like when it comes to budgeting, for example, which is completely customizable based on your needs. Since Instagram's advertising runs on the same platform as Facebook ads manager, what happens with the daily budget is that Facebook will spend a fixed or designated amount to help you deliver your ads each day on the campaign dates that you selected. The lifetime budget option lets you choose the amount you would be willing to spend during the dates of your ad campaign. Once you've chosen your budget, you will then select the schedule for which your ad will run. This will depend on the timeframe which you have set when you were planning the campaign in the initial stages. It is recommended that you choose the option on Instagram that states *run my ad continuously starting today* if you are looking to build brand awareness.

- **Step 6: Ad Format Selection** - Once you're done setting your budget, schedule and deciding on who your target audience is, the next step of the process is to choose the Instagram ad format that you are going to go with. If you're on a tight budget, you're going to want to take your time carefully selecting the best ad format, so you get the most out of it. Different ad formats will produce different results, and with Instagram, the six different types of ad formats that you get to choose from are Carousel Ads, Single Image Ads, Single Video Ads, Slideshow, Instagram Stories Single Video, and Instagram Stories Single Image.

- **Step 7: Launch Campaigns with A Cause** - Customers want to see that a brand is more than just focused on making sales and profits. They want to see that your brand cares about something other than its sales figures. A campaign that showcases your brand caring for a cause is a good way to shine the spotlight on your business. Your campaign for a cause should be a cause that your audiences will be able to relate to, something that resonates with them. For example, Dove launched its #DoveWithoutCruelty campaign, which emphasized the brand's commitment to not test its products on animals. Dove partnered with PETA and other social media influencers to promote this cause and it resonated well with a lot of other Instagrammers out there.

## Maximizing Your Marketing Campaign Potential

Instagram has made it easier than ever for businesses to sell their products and services on social media. Social media marketing today is not an option anymore. It's a *necessity*. Conventional advertising methods are slowly on their way out. If you want your business to get noticed, you need to be on social media. It's safe to say that every second you're not on social media is another second which is wasted because you could have been improving your brand awareness and driving sales.

Consumers these days prefer online shopping more than any other shopping method. The convenience that comes with online shopping is a huge incentive, and when these consumers are easily able to reach out and contact the brand, that motivates them even more because of the customer service experience that they receive. Powerful marketing campaigns help nudge your consumers in the direction to take action. While there may not be any sure-fire guarantees, what you can guarantee is that if you do the best that you can to ensure you're maximizing your campaign's potential, you stand a good chance of coming out on top.

- **Be Short, Move Fast** - Social media is a fast-moving platform, and Instagram is no different. Customers spend only seconds on an image or video before losing interest and moving onto the next. They come here for the visuals and the videos, and they *don't* want to do a lot of reading. Keep your content to a maximum of 40 characters and nothing more, Instagram is the ideal example of a platform where less is more, in this case, especially when it comes to texts and words.

- **The Power Lies in Your Visuals** - Not just images, but high-quality video content, too. Fantastic photos are what Instagram is all about. If you want to bring in the sales, boost your brand's reputation, and grab the attention of new customers, high-quality images need to be your no-break rule for every piece of content you produce with each marketing campaign. Customers these days are not about the hard sell anymore; they want something that is genuine and authentic to look at.

- **Don't Overshadow Your Product** - A good rule of thumb to follow is that your branding should not be overshadowing your product. If it is, then you probably need to scale back on the branding a little bit. While you do need to feature your brand and logo on every content your produce, you may need to do it in a subtle manner so it doesn't appear like a "direct sales pitch" or hard sell.

- **Working Landing Pages** - Customers will be extremely put off when they arrive at your landing page only to run into technical issues. All that hard work you put into your campaign is going to be futile if your landing page falls short since the customer won't be able to complete the final purchase anyway. Always test to make sure your landing pages are in working order so no one is left disappointed at the end of the day.

- **Testing 1, 2, 3...** - Run a couple of "test ads" on your Instagram stories and profile to see how your audience responds to it. Do they like your content enough to engage with it? Or is it not getting the response that you hope for at all? If it is the latter, it might be worth reconsidering if you'll want to spend money on this campaign. Test runs are a good indicator of whether your full-fledged campaign is going to work the way that you intend it to, which could end up saving you wasted money.

- **Never Forget Your Call-to-Action -** The whole reason you're running this advertising campaign in the first place is because you want to see some real sales results. Without proper call-to-action, your customers are not going to know what needs to be done next. A call-to-action prompts and reminds them what the "next step" should be. *Shop now, sign up now, apply now, contact us now, watch now, and download now* are some examples of a call-to-action you should be using, depending on the nature of your campaign.

**Common Marketing Mistakes**

Instagram, in many ways, is a great platform for businesses to share their creativity while building a connection and a lasting relationship with their customers. For the inexperienced marketer though, there's a lot of potentials for risky mistakes to be made. Even experienced marketers could fall prey to social media marketing faux pas on Instagram that could kill the sales of your business. Some mistakes on social media could end up becoming costly affairs, bringing all that success and momentum you've built to a halt if you're not careful.

While sometimes mistakes do happen despite your best efforts, it's still best to avoid them altogether if you can. Mistakes can be learning opportunities, but sometimes, those lessons could cost you more than you bargained for. Where possible, you want to minimize the mistakes to maximize the potential. Let's look at some of the common marketing pitfalls that get made on Instagram:

- **Mistake #1: Buying Followers** - As thrilling as it is to see your Instagram following quickly climb to an impressive count, you're setting yourself up for trouble if you give in to temptation and start buying followers. This isn't just a mistake, it's almost like committing fraud. Fake followers have become such a serious thing that brands have started adding it to their contracts drawn up with influencers. Not only do you run the risk of harming the reputation of your brand by discrediting it, but there are also real legal consequences which you might have to contend with. Since these followers are fake, your return on investment is still going to underperform anyway, since no real sales can be made. Customers might not trust your credibility again, and for a business, this is a very serious issue indeed.

- **Mistake #2: A Lack of Engagement** - Avoid treating Instagram as merely a platform for you to sell your content because that's not all that it is, and treating it as such is only going to lose you followers in the long run. Failing to engage enough with your customers is another mistake that a lot of marketers tend to make. Customers expect you to be responsive to their queries or comments, and the quicker you are to reply, the happier they will be. If all you do is sell, sell, sell, and ignore them, it won't be long before they turn away from you and head right to your competitors.

- **Mistake #3: Only Relying on Images** - It may be an image-centric platform, but with the other available ad options which have been introduced, there is no reason for businesses to just stick to one source of promoting their content. Customers are going to be bored very quickly with monotony. Avoid limiting your advertising potential to just one content source and don't be afraid to experiment and play around with the other options.

- **Mistake #4: You're Rushing** - Getting so caught up in just trying to dole out content regularly to remain active on Instagram that you forget or overlook the quality aspect of it all is another frequent mistake that gets made. This mistake can pose a challenge because, on the one hand, you need fresh content daily so your customers don't forget you exist. But on the other hand, trying to come up with ideas for quality content every day is not such an easy task either. Every now and then, you will experience the occasional mental block and be completely stuck for ideas on what to do next. The stress of publishing daily could cause a lot of businesses to rush and post less than perfect material. Forgetting a call-to-action, missing some hashtags, and a description that doesn't quite match your content are some examples of what could go wrong when you rush before you're ready.

- **Mistake #5: Inconsistent Frequency** - If you post too much, you run the risk of spamming your customer's newsfeed. But then again, if there's too big a gap between your last post, you're at risk of appearing like an inconsistent or inactive business profile. You don't want to be one of those businesses that post a ridiculous amount of content until your customers get tired of it, but neither do you want your postings to be so sparse your customers wonder if you're even active on social media anymore. It's a fine line to balance, but it is a great example of why you should never ignore your analytics. The less information you have to work with, the more susceptible you will be to committing errors.

- **Mistake #6: Forgetting Your Captions** - An oversight that a lot of marketers end up making when they think Instagram is all about the visuals. That captions are secondary and don't matter as much. Captions may not be as long or descriptive as they are on Facebook or other social media platforms, but they still *do matter*. A well-composed caption has always been a crucial part of starting conversations on social media. You need great captions to cement the point that you're trying to make, and without them, your visuals simply may not be powerful enough to tell the story that you want to be heard.

- **Mistake #7: No Concrete Goals to Guide You** - It cannot be emphasized enough how important goals are to success. Every campaign that you plan *must have goals*, you simply cannot achieve the level of success you want without setting a goal that is going to point you in the right direction. Without setting proper goals, you leave your campaign open and vulnerable to mistakes getting made more frequently than ever. Remember how having no goals is like shooting in the dark and hoping you'll get lucky? This can turn out to be a very costly mistake when you're ill-equipped to deal with the challenges that are going to come along the way when running your ad campaign. If you aren't clear about what the aim of your ad is, you'll never know if what you're doing is working or not.

**Best Instagram Marketing Tips**

We've become so used to seeing ads on our newsfeed these days that it feels like they have been around forever. Each day, as you scroll through any of your social media platforms (not just Instagram alone), within a minute or two, you're bound to encounter an ad. Maybe even within seconds of scrolling through your newsfeed, that's how common they have become. They may have been around for some time now, but businesses are still figuring it out, experimenting to see what works best, trying different tools and tactics as they get a feel for the feature, and determining what's going to work best for their business. There's always something new to be learned and discovered, as these social media platforms themselves continuously work to improve.

One of the reasons why navigating social media platforms is an ongoing learning process is because not every platform works in the same way. They each come with their own set of strengths, advantages, all of which can be used to help benefit a business's overall campaign goals. Instagram is no different. Being a platform which is all about the visuals, Instagram is unique because it offers advertisers an outlet for them to get inspired. To discover new, creative possibilities and to bring those discoveries to their brand as they continue working diligently to enhance the experience of their audience and customers. Being an image-focused (and now video too) platform, first and foremost, Instagram hasn't lost its touch and stays true to that concept even through their ad offerings. They know it's because this is what the viewers have come to expect, what they have become accustomed to.

To get the most out of your marketing efforts on this platform, you need to position yourself one step ahead of your customer. Anticipate their needs, figure out what they want even *before* they do. Managing a social media marketing campaign is hard work, but there are certain tips and tricks you could take your profile, marketing, and advertising efforts from good to better, and finally, to *exceptional.*

- ***Tip #1 - All Your Liked Photos In One Place***. Did you know that there's a quick way to view all the posts you've liked on Instagram in one place? Go to the "Options" tab, and then click on the "Posts You've Liked" selection. If you want to unlike any of them, just tap on the image and unlike the content. Don't worry, the user won't be notified that you've stopped liking their content.

- ***Tip #2 - Saving What You Love.*** View all your most-loved content and save them for easy viewing later on by simply bookmarking them. On your profile, you will notice that there is a bookmark icon at the top-right above your images. Tap on it, and select the "Collections" tab. If you haven't created one yet, simply select the "Create Collection" and start saving all your favorite content.

- ***Tip #3 - The H.D.D (Hide, Disable, Delete)*** - Good business practice would be to *not* disable comments on your profile because this is one of your means of communication with your audience and customer base. However, if you do have to hide it, delete it, or even disable commenting for any reason, here's what you would need to do. Head on over to your "Options" tab once more, and then select on "Comments". Once you've done that, you'll have the option of filtering through your comments based on the keywords. Try toggling "Hide Inappropriate Comments" and key in the specific keywords which you're after so you can keep an eye out for comments that may not be the best fit for your profile. To delete comments, you'll need to head over to the speech bubble icon, which is located below the comment that you're looking to delete. You will then need to swipe to the left. There'll be a "trash can" icon that appears after you do this, and by tapping on that, your comment will be gone. If you're wondering whether you can disable comments entirely across your profile, the answer is no. Unfortunately, disabling needs to be done for each individual post. If you've got a post you don't want people commenting on, use the "Advanced Settings" option before you post your content. Choose the "Turn Off Commenting" option and no one will be able to post any comments on that particular post.

- ***Tip #5 - That Extra Special Font.*** There are always ways to make your profile stand out, one of which is by using special fonts. Ordinary keyboard typing limits your creativity because there's only one option to go with - whatever the keyboard presents you with. As always, third-party solution providers come to the rescue, and all you need to do is head over to these websites and copy special fonts from there. These fonts are not often found with Instagram and its community, so when you utilize these fonts, your profile will really stand out and be memorable. Websites like Instagram Fonts and LingoJam are a good place to start.

- ***Tip #6 - Stay "Fresh" Without Deleting.*** Delete all your old, outdated content *without actually removing any* of them from your profile. This keeps your profile looking fresh, updated, and always on-trend, the way your customers expect it to. Head to the post which you want to "remove" and then tap on the three dots at the top of the post. Next, select the "Archive" option to archive the content. You can review your archived content anytime by selecting the "Archive" icon, which is located at the top right corner of your profile page.

# Conclusion

Thank you for making it through to the end of *Instagram Marketing: The Ultimate Guide for Social Media Success*. Let's hope it was informative and able to provide you with all the tools you need to achieve your goals whatever they may be.

Understanding the dynamics of how Instagram, as both a social media platform *and* a marketing tool, works is the way to get the most out of your marketing efforts. Every content crafted needs to be tailored to fit the specific dynamics of the platform. That's how you leverage Instagram to its fullest advantage. Instagram's popularity and potential have become so hard to ignore that if you're not on the platform, you're losing out as a business.

It's always challenging in the beginning, but the best social media marketing advice you can take away with you is to find what works best for your individual business needs and go with that. You don't need to follow another company's marketing campaign or strategy just because it was successful. What worked for them might not be the right approach for you; your business goals and needs are unique. As such, you need to figure out the approach that's going to be most beneficial *for your business and no one else's*. It might take some trial and error in the beginning, but you'll get there eventually.

Instagram is going to be around for a very long time, and it's only going to get *bigger and better*. Instagram is loved by businesses and marketers, and it is easy to see why. Every business wants to make an impression on Instagram. Every business wants to be remembered, and every business wants to leave its mark among the millions (and counting) of Instagrammers out there on the platform in the hopes of making more sales. Every single user on Instagram right now is a potential customer. That's an opportunity that no business can afford to pass up.

Instagram is a social media platform unlike any other. 2 million global advertisers and 25 million businesses have experienced all the benefits that came with marketing themselves on Instagram. Yours could be next.

Finally, if you found this book useful in any way, a review on Amazon is always appreciated!

www.ingramcontent.com/pod-product-compliance
Lightning Source LLC
Chambersburg PA
CBHW070417220526
45466CB00004B/1447